Curriculum Visions

Jewish
faith and practice

Items used in Jewish worship.

Brian Knapp and Lisa Magloff

The Jewish faith

Faith can be described as believing in certain things with mind, heart and soul; and then living by them in the course of everyday life. Faith is always personal. Each person must believe for themselves. Here are some main parts of the Jewish faith.

Jewish beliefs

▶ There is only One God and Creator, who cannot be seen or described.

▶ Prayers should be said to God and only to God.

▶ God knows the thoughts and deeds of all people.

▶ God made a unique covenant, or agreement, with the Jewish people.

▶ One of the greatest leaders of the ancient Jewish people was Moses. God gave laws to Moses on Mount Sinai. These laws include the Ten Commandments.

▶ The Jewish Bible includes the writings of Moses, called the Torah. It also includes writings by prophets and kings, as well as proverbs and Psalms. Jewish scriptures also include writings made by scholars over a long period of time.

▶ A man named Abraham was one of the founders of the Jewish faith. He had a special covenant with God.

▶ God promised Abraham and his descendants that they would live in the Promised Land. This land is ancient Israel.

▶ Jewish scripture teaches us that we must all work to make the world a perfect place.

▶ Judaism is not just a set of beliefs and practices, it is a way of living life. Judaism is filled with practices and traditions that affect every aspect of life.

▶ Many of the laws in the Jewish Bible teach us how to help make the world a perfect place. They include ideas like having compassion for all living things, and striving towards peace.

Find out more

Look at the companion Curriculum Visions book, 'Jewish synagogue'.

Contents

As you go through the book, look for words in **BOLD CAPITALS**. These words are defined in the glossary.

⚠ Understanding others

Remember that other people's beliefs are important to them. You must always be considerate and understanding when studying about faith.

Undressing the Torah scroll.

What it means to be Jewish

Being a Jew means having a unique relationship with God, and also being a member of the Jewish nation.

JUDAISM is more than 4,000 years old and is one of the oldest of the world's faiths. However, Judaism is more than a faith.

Any person born to a Jewish mother or who converts to Judaism is considered to be a JEW, even if they never practise the Jewish religion. In this sense, Judaism is a bit like citizenship, and Jews often describe themselves as part of the 'Jewish nation' or 'Jewish people'.

Origins of Judaism

Jewish history began with a nomadic people who lived near ancient Sumeria, in what we now call the MIDDLE EAST. These people originally believed in many gods, but eventually a man named ABRAHAM began to believe in just one supreme God.

The Jewish scriptures tell how God made an agreement (called a COVENANT) with Abraham, promising that he would be the father of a great nation. In return, Abraham and his descendants would have to show God their faith and obedience. This agreement with God is the basis for the Jewish faith.

Jewish beliefs

Jewish beliefs focus on creating a just and perfect world. The centre of this is our relationship with God and with each other. Judaism involves worship, but it also involves things such as working for justice and caring for the environment.

The Jewish scriptures discuss the obligations, called COMMANDMENTS or MITZVOT, that are important to achieving a just and perfect world. For example, some commandments show us how to worship God in synagogue and in everyday life,

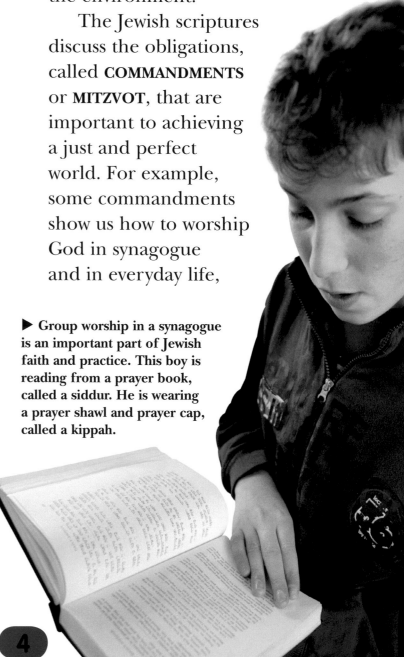

▶ Group worship in a synagogue is an important part of Jewish faith and practice. This boy is reading from a prayer book, called a siddur. He is wearing a prayer shawl and prayer cap, called a kippah.

> **Atonement**
>
> Judaism teaches that people are born with tendencies to do both good and bad and have free will to choose which of these paths to follow. If people choose unwisely, they can repent (atone) for their bad behaviour and acts (their sins). In this way, Judaism shows us that there is always a 'way back' to God.

while others show us how to treat all the other people in our lives.

One God

At the heart of Jewish belief is the idea that there is only one God, that God is everywhere and created everything, and that God cannot be divided into parts or described. This can be seen in one of the most important Jewish prayers, called the **SHEMA**, which says, in part: "The Lord is our God, The Lord is One".

Jewish values

Jewish scriptures also help teach us how to live a good and honest life. Some of the values discussed in the scriptures are: that all life is important, the importance of justice and equality, showing kindness and generosity, the importance of education and social responsibility.

A perfect world

Jewish scripture teaches that one day the world will be a perfect place, but that God will not bring this about unless we first work for it. So, it is up to every person to work to bring about a perfect world.

▲ This stained glass window from a synagogue shows several symbols which are important in Judaism: an Israeli flag, a TORAH scroll, a MENORAH, and a man blowing a SHOFAR outside the walls of Jerusalem. The olive branch and menorah are emblems of Israel.

Weblink: www.CurriculumVisions.com

Jewish roots

The Jewish faith traces its roots back to the PROPHET Abraham.

There is no one founder of Judaism. Over time, God gave the principles of Jewish belief to different people, starting with Abraham. So, knowing the history of Abraham and his descendants is very important in Judaism.

Abraham

According to Jewish tradition, Abraham was born in the city of Ur in **BABYLON**. He was the son of an **IDOL** merchant, but from his early childhood, Abraham questioned the faith of his father. He came to believe that the entire universe was the work of a single Creator, and he began to teach this belief to others.

Abraham tried to convince his father, Terach, of the folly of idol worship. One day, when Abraham was left alone to mind the store, he took a hammer and smashed all of the idols except the largest one. Then he placed the hammer in the hand of the largest idol. When his father returned and asked Abraham what happened, he said, "The idols got into a fight, and the big one smashed all the other ones." His father said, "Don't be ridiculous. These idols aren't alive, they can't do anything." Abraham replied, "Then why do you worship them?"

▲ God tested Abraham's faith by asking Abraham to sacrifice his son. Abraham had so much faith in God that he agreed to do it. But at the last minute, God sent an angel to stop the sacrifice and allowed Abraham to sacrifice a sheep instead.

Eventually, God called to Abraham, telling him to leave his father's home and put his faith in God. God then showed Abraham the land that he would live in – the **PROMISED LAND**. Abraham did as God said. He left his home and travelled for many years, to the land that would later be called **ISRAEL**. He married Sarah and they had a son, named Isaac.

Isaac

God commanded Abraham to sacrifice Isaac as a sign of his faith. Abraham agreed, but at the last moment God sent an **ANGEL** to stop the sacrifice. Isaac later married Rebecca, and they had twin sons: Jacob and Esau.

Jacob (Israel)

Jacob and his brother Esau were very different. Esau hated Jacob and forced him to flee and live with his uncle.

Jacob later had 12 sons and one daughter and eventually decided to return home to his father's land.

The night before he went to meet his brother, Jacob sent his family and things ahead. That night, he wrestled with a man until the break of day. As the dawn broke, Jacob demanded a blessing from the man, and the 'man' revealed himself as a messenger from God. He blessed Jacob and gave him the name 'Israel', meaning 'Champion of God' (this is why, after this, the descendants of Jacob are called the Children of Israel, or **ISRAELITES**). The next day Esau welcomed Jacob (now Israel) home and he became a great leader of his people.

The children of Israel

Abraham, Isaac and Jacob (Israel) are called the **PATRIARCHS**, or fathers, of Judaism.

Jacob's 12 sons became the leaders of 12 families. These families, the descendants of Israel (Jacob) would grow and eventually become what we today call the Jewish people.

Jacob's favourite son was Joseph, who had dreams that he would one day be a great leader. Joseph's older brothers were jealous of him and sold Joseph into slavery in Egypt.

Joseph's ability to know the meaning of dreams earned him a respected position in Egypt. Later, Joseph's family and many other Israelites came to Egypt to escape a famine.

◄► Joseph dreamed that he and his brothers were in the fields at harvest time and were tying up sheaves of wheat. Joseph's sheaf stood upright, while his brothers' sheaves bowed down to it. Joseph then dreamed that the Sun and the Moon and eleven stars were all bowing down to him. When Joseph's brothers heard these dreams, they became very angry and jealous and sold Joseph into slavery in Egypt.

The Exodus and the giving of the Torah

As centuries passed, the Jews in Egypt became slaves and suffered under the Pharaohs (the kings of Egypt). So God chose Moses to lead the Israelites out of Egypt and into the land that God had promised to Abraham's descendants – called Canaan, Israel, or the **PROMISED LAND**.

▶ Moses led the Israelites to the Promised Land, but he died before setting foot on it. Just before he died, God took Moses to the top of a mountain and showed him the Promised Land. This stained glass window shows Moses looking at the Promised Land.

▼ The Pharaoh let the Israelites leave Egypt after God had sent TEN PLAGUES to Egypt. God parted the Red Sea so the Israelites could flee. After escaping from Egypt, the Israelites wandered in the Sinai desert for 40 years. For all this time, Moses led the Israelites, but he was guided and helped by God.

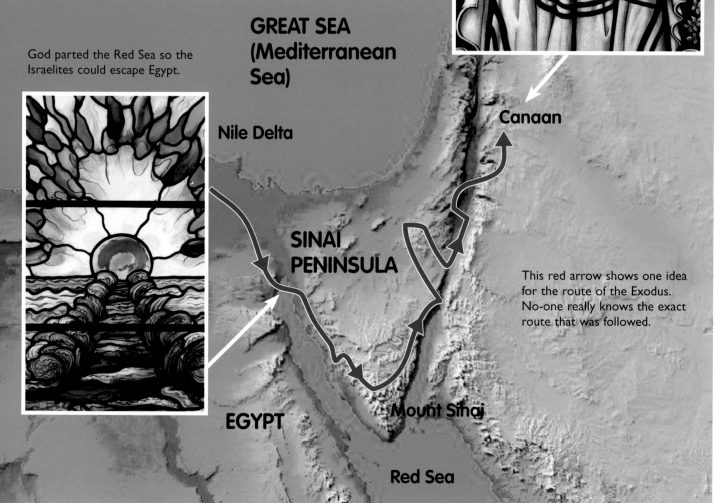

God parted the Red Sea so the Israelites could escape Egypt.

GREAT SEA (Mediterranean Sea)

Nile Delta

Canaan

SINAI PENINSULA

This red arrow shows one idea for the route of the Exodus. No-one really knows the exact route that was followed.

EGYPT

Mount Sinai

Red Sea

God led the Israelites out of Egypt and through the wilderness to Mount Sinai. God then gave the Israelites a set of laws to follow, which included the TEN COMMANDMENTS.

After 40 more years of wandering in the desert, the Israelites reached a place called CANAAN, where they settled. Each of the 12 families was given a part of Canaan to settle in and Canaan became the 'land of the Israelites', or ancient Israel.

The land of Israel

Over the following centuries, Israel was ruled by kings. One of the most important of these was King David, who made Jerusalem the capital. David's son, King Solomon, built the first Temple at Jerusalem. For hundreds of years, THE TEMPLE was the centre of the Jewish religion and the place where the most sacred ceremonies of Judaism were practised.

▲ This stained glass window shows the ancient Temple in Jerusalem. Inside The Temple were kept the original Ten Commandments. This is where sacred ceremonies were performed. The remains of the Western Wall can be seen today.

The rule of the kings of Israel was not always peaceful. The land was conquered and reconquered several times, and the original Temple was destroyed and rebuilt. Eventually, the ancient Romans conquered Israel (which they called JUDEA) in 63 BCE. The Romans treated the Jews cruelly and the Jewish people rebelled against Roman rule.

The diaspora

In 70 CE, after a huge Jewish revolt, the Romans tore down The Temple, and forbade any Jews from living in, or even entering, Jerusalem. The Romans also renamed Judea, calling it Palestine, and many Jews were taken to Rome as slaves. Most of the Jewish people were now forced to leave Israel to live elsewhere. This is the start of the DIASPORA, or dispersion.

Over the next 1,900 years, the Jewish people spread out around the world. During this time, the dream of returning to the Promised Land was kept alive. In 1948, the modern state of Israel was formed, and many Jews from around the world came to live there.

Weblink: www.CurriculumVisions.com

Jewish holy books

The Jewish scriptures were given to Moses by God. They include many commandments.

The Jewish Bible

Jews base their faith on the word of God as told to Moses. God spoke to Moses and Moses wrote down God's word. This is the first, holiest part of the Jewish Bible and is called the **FIVE BOOKS OF MOSES**, or the **TORAH** (Law).

These books contain a history of the Jewish people from the creation of the world to the death of Moses. They also contain rules and laws about how to live. (The Ten Commandments are part of these.)

These five books are called Genesis, Exodus, Leviticus, Numbers and Deuteronomy. Some of the stories you will find here include

▲ The precious scrolls can easily be damaged from oils in our hands, so a pointer, called a YAD, is used while reading, instead of a finger.

▼ Reading the Torah aloud is an important part of Jewish worship. The Torah that is read in SYNAGOGUE is written by hand, in Hebrew, on scrolls made from parchment. The entire Torah is read during worship over the course of a year. This boy is reading the Torah aloud during worship. He is wearing a prayer shawl, called a TALLIT, and a prayer cap called a KIPPAH.

▲ The Torah scrolls are kept in a special cabinet called an ARK. They are also covered with specially decorated cloth covers and 'dressed' with silver decorations. The covers and decorations help to protect the valuable scrolls, and are also reminders of how priests in the ancient Temple in Jerusalem used to dress.

Where the word Tanakh comes from

The word Tanakh comes from the three types of scriptures that make up the Tanakh: Torah (T), Nevi'im (N) and Ketuvim (K).

Hebrew, like Arabic, consists of groups of consonants, with vowels written above the word. Usually, the vowels are left out of written Hebrew, so the word Tanakh is spelled tnk.

the Garden of Eden, Noah and the flood, and Joseph and his coat of many colours.

The Jewish Bible also includes other writings, such as the writings of the prophets, proverbs, Psalms and other stories. These are collected in two books called Prophets (Nevi'im) and Writings (Ketuvim). Together, the Torah, Prophets and Writings are called the **TANAKH**, or written scripture.

Christians call these books the Old Testament. The books that Christians call the New Testament are not part of Jewish scripture.

Talmud

Over time, scholars studied how to apply the commandments and laws to their changing lives. These studies were passed on from one generation to the next by word of mouth, so it is called the Spoken Torah, or **ORAL TORAH**. The Oral Torah was passed down from generation to generation and finally written down in a book called the **MISHNAH**.

Over time, many scholars added their ideas and comments to the Mishnah. These extra comments were also written down, in a book called the **GEMARA**. Together, the Mishnah and the Gemara are called the **TALMUD**.

The Talmud tells Jews how to apply God's commandments in all the different situations of everyday life.

Weblink: www.CurriculumVisions.com

Judaism in everyday life

For many Jews, Jewish law affects every aspect of everyday life.

▲ This plaque above the Ark in a synagogue contains the first words of each of the Ten Commandments.

Judaism is not just a set of beliefs about God, man and the universe. Judaism is also filled with practices and traditions that affect every aspect of life.

Path of life

Many Jews follow a set of rules and guidelines known as **HALAKHAH**, which govern every aspect of their lives.

The word 'halakhah' is a Hebrew word which means to go, to walk or to travel. So, although halakhah is usually translated as 'Jewish Law', it also means 'the path that one walks'.

The 613 Mitzvot

At the heart of halakhah are the commandments, or mitzvot, found in the Torah. These are the laws which God expects Jews to follow.

Some of the mitzvot describe what types of food can and cannot be eaten, how and when to pray, how to observe the **SHABBAT**, how to try legal cases, how to treat others, and how to live a good and moral life.

Some of the mitzvot are in the Bible, such as honouring our parents, being kind to animals and looking after the poor. Other mitzvot are customs that have been discussed by scholars for centuries. For example, the mitzvah (singular of mitzvot) to recite grace after meals comes from the sentence in the Bible: "and you will eat and be satisfied and bless the Lord your God".

The story of Hillel

This story is a good example of the most important part of halakhah:

Hillel was a very famous Jewish scholar who lived in the first century BCE.

One day a non-Jew came to Hillel's house, intending to make fun of his beliefs. He said to Hillel, "Teach me the Torah while I am standing on one foot." Hillel responded. "No problem! The main idea of the Torah is 'Love your neighbour as yourself.' Now, if you're really interested, you can go and study more." The man was so impressed with Hillel's response, that he began to study the Torah seriously, and became a Jew.

Food laws

KASHRUT is the part of Jewish law that deals with what foods can and cannot be eaten, and how those foods must be prepared. The word Kashrut means fit, proper or correct.

Food that follows Kashrut laws is called **KOSHER**.

Kosher is not a style of cooking and so any type of cooking can be kosher. There are many Kashrut laws, but simply, any animal that has cloven hooves and chews its cud is kosher. So, for example, lamb and beef are kosher, but pork isn't. Also, any seafood that has fins and scales is kosher. So, salmon and herring are kosher, but shellfish is not kosher.

Also, meat cannot be eaten in the same meal as dairy (milk, cheese and eggs).

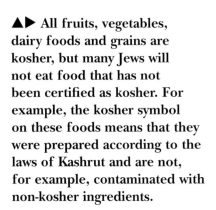

▲▶ All fruits, vegetables, dairy foods and grains are kosher, but many Jews will not eat food that has not been certified as kosher. For example, the kosher symbol on these foods means that they were prepared according to the laws of Kashrut and are not, for example, contaminated with non-kosher ingredients.

Prayer

Prayer is the core of Jewish religious life.

The Hebrew word for prayer is tefillah, which means 'to judge yourself'. This is why the most important part of Jewish prayer is to give time to look inside ourselves, to examine our role in the universe and our relationship to God.

For an observant Jew, prayer is part of everyday life. There are blessings to recite when performing any mitzvah, such as before lighting candles on the Sabbath, before eating certain types of food and after a meal, to thank God for the food.

All of these prayers are in addition to formal worship services in the synagogue.

Hebrew

The Talmud says that Jews can pray in any language that they can understand, but traditionally Jews have always prayed in **HEBREW**, and most Jewish children learn Hebrew so that they can understand the prayers they say, as well as read the Torah in its original form.

▼ A congregation during service. Some prayers are said by the entire congregation, often when standing.

▼ Learning Hebrew is important in the Jewish faith.

Praying together

While many prayers and blessings are meant to be said throughout the day, group worship services in the synagogue are also important.

In some synagogues, group prayer services are held three times each day, in the evening, morning and afternoon. In some Jewish traditions a fourth daily service is added on the Sabbath and on Jewish holidays.

During service many different prayers are said and Psalms are sung. All the prayers are written down in a prayer book called a **SIDDUR**.

Usually, the prayers in the siddur are written in both Hebrew and the local language (in England, it would be English).

God is One

The oldest daily prayer in Judaism is called the Shema. The Shema begins, "Hear, O Israel: The Lord is our God, The Lord is One." It is recited at every service.

One important part of daily prayer services is the **AMIDAH** (meaning standing, because it is recited while standing), or Tefillah (meaning The Prayer, because it is the essence of all Jewish prayer).

▼ These children are reading prayers from their prayer book, or siddur.

▼ In this picture a rabbi is leading a group prayer during worship services. The rabbi may also give a talk, or sermon, which explains the part of the Torah that was read aloud.

It consists of 18 blessings, such as blessings for healing the sick, peace on Earth and blessings in praise of God. The Amidah is sometimes called the **SHEMONEH ESREI** (18) prayer. It is the cornerstone of every Jewish service.

Most Jews stand facing the Ark (in Hebrew **ARON KODESH**, the cabinet that houses the Torah scrolls) while reciting the Amidah. The Ark is always on the east wall of the synagogue, so the congregation faces Jerusalem during worship.

An important part of Sabbath prayer services is a reading from the Torah and the Prophets. The Torah has been divided into sections, and one section is read each week, so

that the entire Torah is read each year. The Torah sections are always read in the same order, so every synagogue in the world reads the same section on the same week.

The Torah is read in synagogue on the Sabbath and on some holidays. In some traditions, it is also read during services on Mondays and Thursdays. The Torah readings are performed with great ceremony: the Torah is paraded around the room before it is brought to rest on the **BIMAH** (podium), and it is considered an honour to have the opportunity to recite a blessing over the reading (this honour is called an aliyah).

On Shabbat and holidays, services also include reading and singing Psalms and a talk by the rabbi on the Torah reading or another important topic.

At the end of every service, a prayer called Aleinu, which praises God, is recited. This is followed by singing Psalms.

Taking part

During worship service, some prayers and blessings are said by each person to themselves, other prayers are read aloud. At certain times, worshippers are expected to stand up or bow, for example when the doors of the Ark are opened, in order to show respect.

Weblink: www.CurriculumVisions.com

Shabbat

This is the Jewish day of rest.

The word Shabbat is the Hebrew word for Sabbath. The word Shabbat means 'to rest' and the Shabbat is primarily a day of rest and spiritual enrichment.

The story of how Shabbat came about is given in **EXODUS** 31:16–17, "Wherefore the children of Israel shall keep the Sabbath, to observe the Sabbath throughout their generations, for a perpetual covenant (promise). It is a sign between God and the children of Israel forever; for in six days the Lord made heaven and earth, and on the seventh day God ceased from work and rested." So, by resting on the seventh day, we remember and acknowledge the covenant God made with Israel and that God is the creator of Heaven and Earth and all living things.

The Sabbath is not only a day where no work is done, it is a time to think, to study the Torah, to be with our families and to become closer to God.

Sunset to sunset

Shabbat begins before sunset on Friday. Because Shabbat is a time of rest, there are a great many things that are not allowed on Shabbat, such as working, lighting fires and handling money.

▲ A stained glass window from a synagogue showing a traditional Shabbat meal.

Shabbat is celebrated both at home and in synagogue. At sunset, two Shabbat candles are lit. Before dinner a prayer called **KIDDUSH** is recited by the family. This prayer is said over a glass of wine and sanctifies, or makes holy, the Sabbath. The family also says blessings together and then eats a meal together. In some traditions, the meal starts with a type of braided bread, called hallah.

The next morning, there are special Shabbat services in the synagogue. These may include readings from the Tanakh and also a sermon or talk by the **RABBI**.

The rabbi may discuss the Torah and what it means, and he or she may discuss how the part of the Torah that was read fits in with modern life or current events.

End of Shabbat

Shabbat ends at sunset on Saturday. At the end of Shabbat, the family says special prayers and blessings over wine, sweet smelling spices and candles. These blessings are called HAVDALAH (separation). They are a reminder of the difference between Shabbat and other days of the week.

Before the Shabbat meal, candles are lit and special blessings are said. These are usually done by an adult woman of the family. In the inset, the father of the family is cutting a slice of hallah. This is a type of bread made by twisting the dough into a braid. Hallah is a traditional way to start the Shabbat meal.

Weblink: www.CurriculumVisions.com

Rabbis and chazans

Rabbis are the clergy of the Jewish faith.

In the synagogue, worship services are often led by the **RABBI**. A rabbi is not a priest but is more like a teacher and a spiritual leader. In some Jewish traditions only men are rabbis, while in others both men and women can be rabbis.

Rabbis

In Judaism, any adult who knows Hebrew and who knows how, can lead worship services. At home, daily prayers and blessings are said by a member of the family. However, most worship services in the synagogue are led by the rabbi.

A rabbi is a spiritual leader of the Jewish community, in much the same way as a Protestant minister, ministering to the community, leading community religious services and dealing with many of the administrative matters related to the synagogue.

The word rabbi means teacher, and the rabbi is also a teacher. All rabbis have spent many years studying Jewish law and the Torah and Talmud.

The rabbi organises and leads worship services, and may give a sermon or talk. But the rabbi's job involves many other functions.

▼ Any adult who knows the Torah well may lead worship services in the synagogue.

◄ A rabbi is a teacher and a leader of the religious community. Rabbis go to school in order to learn about the Torah and the Talmud, and how to teach and counsel in religious matters.

Chazan

Music and song are very important parts of worship in the synagogue. So, some synagogues have a chazan (pronounced ha-zan), or **CANTOR** to lead the chanting and singing of prayers in the synagogue. In some synagogues, this job is done by the rabbi, or a member of the congregation. Or there may be a choir made up of members of the community.

Large synagogues may employ a professional chazan, who has studied music, the Hebrew language and the Jewish religion for many years. The chazan may also conduct weddings and funerals and do some other jobs to help the rabbi. The rabbi and chazan work as partners to educate and inspire the congregation.

Warden

A warden, or gabbai, is a person who volunteers to help make sure that everything is ready for the service, and that the service runs smoothly. Serving as a warden is a great honour.

These include: instructing the adults and children of the community in the Jewish religion; answering questions and resolving disputes regarding Jewish law and religion; performing marriages and funerals; and pastoral duties, such as helping people who have problems.

When giving a sermon, the rabbi will try to make his or her sermon clear and understandable to everyone, even to children, and he or she may use humour or stories to help with this.

Weblink: www.CurriculumVisions.com

Jewish symbols in everyday life

Over the years, some symbols have become important to the Jewish faith.

As the Jewish people spread out around the world during the diaspora, they adopted the languages, customs and laws of their new homes. At the same time, Jews adopted symbols and customs that have helped them to keep their faith.

Kippah

The **KIPPAH** (pronounced key-pah) is a small headcovering.

There is no commandment to wear the kippah, but it was an ancient practice for Jewish men to cover their heads during prayer, in order to show respect for God. Today, many Jews wear the kippah all of the time, as a sign of their faith, to show that they are servants of God, and as a reminder that God is always above us.

Magen David

This six pointed star is called the **MAGEN DAVID**, Star of David or the Shield of David in English.

It is supposed to represent the shape of King David's shield, but has only been a symbol of the Jewish faith since about the 17th century, when it became a popular practice to

◄ A Magen David (Star of David) necklace.

put Magen Davids on the outside of synagogues, to identify them as Jewish houses of worship.

Many Jews in Europe were forced to wear a Magen David on their sleeves as a way to single them out. Later, the Magen David was adopted as a symbol of the new state of Israel and put on the Israeli flag.

►A kippah is always worn in synagogue, but many Jewish men wear one all the time.

▶ The chai is a reminder that life is precious.

Menorah

The **MENORAH** is a seven-branched candlestick and a symbol of the Jewish faith. The ancient Temple in Jerusalem originally contained a golden menorah, which was lit every evening.

The menorah is the oldest symbol of Judaism and of the Jewish mission, given by God, to be "a light unto the nations." (Isaiah 42:6).

In every synagogue, there is a lamp in front of the Ark which is always kept burning. This lamp, called the **NER TAMID** (eternal flame), is a reminder of the menorah in the ancient Temple.

Chai

This symbol (shown above) is often worn on necklaces and other ornaments. It is made up of two letters which spell the Hebrew word for life, Chai. This symbol is a reminder of the importance of life in the Jewish faith.

Mezuzah

Jewish people often place a **MEZUZAH** on the doorposts of their home (the word mezuzah means doorpost). The mezuzah is a constant reminder of God's presence and God's commandments.

▲▼ The symbol on the mezuzah above is the Hebrew letter shin, which stands for the words, 'God Almighty.'

The mezuzah is a small case. Inside is a tiny parchment scroll which contains the words of the Shema prayer. Part of this prayer is the instruction to write God's words on the doorposts of houses.

23

Israel: the promised land

Judaism is closely tied to the state of Israel, the spiritual homeland of the Jewish people.

One of the unique features of Judaism is that the Jewish people believe in a homeland which was given to them by God. Understanding this explains many things about the Jewish religion and how it is practised.

▼ This picture shows the ruins of the Western Wall, which is the only part of the ancient Temple still standing, and the holiest site in Judaism. Behind the wall, you can see the Dome of the Rock, one of the holiest sites in Islam. Jews come to the wall to pray and ask God for guidance.

The Promised Land

Think back to earlier in the book where we said that the history of the Jewish people began when God told Abraham to leave his homeland, promising that, in time, Abraham and his descendants would find a new home in the land of Canaan, now known as Israel. This is why Jews call **ISRAEL** the Promised Land.

After the Romans destroyed The Temple in ancient Jerusalem, Jews dispersed all around the world, but the memory of a homeland in Israel was always kept alive. Many of the Jewish prayers that were used after the diaspora began are about the desire to return to the Promised Land.

The modern state of Israel

During World War II, the Nazis, in Germany, attempted to exterminate the Jewish people from the world. More than 6 million Jews were murdered (along with other people who the Nazis considered to be undesirable). The English word for this tragedy is the **HOLOCAUST**, and the Hebrew word is **SHOAH**.

When World War II ended, Jewish people around the world became convinced that tragedies like the Shoah could never be allowed to happen again. Following a UN vote in 1947, the modern state of Israel was formed in 1948.

▲ For many Jews, Israel is the Promised Land, the land of milk and honey described in the Old Testament.

Jews from all over the world came to live in modern Israel, even though it has not always been peaceful. Some Jews moved to Israel so they could practice their faith in freedom. Others came to Israel because they wanted to be part of a Jewish state.

Weblink: www.CurriculumVisions.com

The Jewish calendar

The Jewish calendar has many festivals and holy days. Some of the most important are the Jewish New Year, Yom Kippur and Passover.

The long history of Judaism has resulted in many festivals and days of commemoration.

The Jewish calendar is lunar, so each month begins on the New Moon. Because of this, the Jewish holidays do not happen on the same day of the solar calendar every year.

In order to keep the calendar lined up with the seasons, a 13th month of 28 days (Adar II) is added every two or three years.

Nissan	30 days	March–April
Iyar	29 days	April–May
Sivan	30 days	May–June
Tammuz	29 days	June–July
Av	30 days	July–August
Elul	29 days	August–September
Tishri	30 days	September–October
Cheshvan	29 or 30 days	October–November
Kislev	29 or 30 days	November–December
Tevet	29 days	December–January
Shevat	30 days	January–February
Adar	29 or 30 days	February–March
Adar II	29 days	March–April

▲ The Jewish calendar is based on the phases of the Moon.

Rosh Hashanah (New Year)

In Hebrew, Rosh Hashanah means 'beginning of the year'. This holiday takes place on the first and second days of the month of Tishri. It is a time of looking back over the past year and thinking about improvements for the future. This is why the Torah calls it a day of remembrance.

On this day a **SHOFAR**, a ram's horn, is blown like a trumpet in the synagogue. The loud, eerie sound is a reminder of God's majesty. During Rosh Hashanah, synagogue services are longer and more solemn than usual, and include prayers of confession and repentance.

▶ One New Year's tradition is to eat apples dipped in honey, for a sweet New Year.

Days of Awe

The ten days in-between Rosh Hashanah and Yom Kippur are called the Days of Awe, or Days of Repentance.

According to Jewish tradition, on Rosh Hashanah, God opens the 'book of life' for the next year, and on Yom Kippur, God seals the book, and our fate for the coming year. This time in-between is a time for thinking about how you can repent for any sins from the past year, and be a better person in the coming year.

During the Days of Awe any disagreements should be resolved. This is a time to apologise to any people you have argued with or who have been hurt by something you have said or done. It is also a time to forgive those who have hurt you.

Yom Kippur

Yom Kippur (Day of Atonement) is probably the most solemn day of the Jewish year.

On this day Jews confess their sins, repent and promise to try and be better people in the year ahead.

For people over 13, Yom Kippur includes a 25-hour fast beginning before sunset and ending after

◀ One extra candle is lit each night during Chanukkah.

nightfall on the day of Yom Kippur. Nothing is eaten or drunk during this time. Many people spend the entire day in prayer in the synagogue.

At the final worship service for Yom Kippur, the Ark remains open, and the shofar is blown at the end of service.

Chanukkah

This is the festival of lights. It is an eight-day festival, beginning on the 25th day of Kislev.

Chanukkah commemorates an event that happened more than 2,000 years ago, at a time when Jews in Israel were ruled by foreign leaders and were not allowed to practise their faith. Judah the Maccabee led a revolt against the foreign rulers and won.

Judah rededicated The Temple, which had been used by the foreign rulers for non-Jewish worship. When he relit the holy lamp, there was only enough oil left for one day, yet by a miracle, the oil lasted for eight days. This is why Chanukkah lasts for eight days.

In the home, each family lights a candle in a special Chanukkah menorah that holds nine candles: one for each night, plus an extra candle which is used to light the others. Each night, an additional candle is lit.

Weblink: www.CurriculumVisions.com

Blessings are said during the lighting, games played, and presents may be given.

Passover (Pesach)

Passover begins on the 14th day of Nissan and lasts for seven days. In some Jewish traditions it lasts for eight days. It celebrates the time when Moses led the Jewish people out of slavery in Egypt and into freedom.

In order to convince the Pharaoh to let the Jewish people go free, God sent ten plagues to Egypt. The final plague was to kill all the Egyptian first-born. The word Pesach means to pass over, or to spare. It refers to the fact that God 'passed over' the houses of the Israelites when he was slaying the first-born of Egypt.

The Jewish people left Egypt in a hurry, and did not have time to let their bread rise and so they took unleavened bread. During Passover, leavened bread is not eaten and a simple unleavened bread, called matzo, is eaten instead.

During Pesach, each family has a special service and meal at home, called a seder. During the seder the story of Passover is told and special foods are eaten which are reminders of the grief of slavery and the joy of freedom. For example, matzo is eaten as a reminder of how the Jews had to leave Egypt in a

▲▶ This boy is playing with a spinning top, called a dreidle, which is a traditional Chanukkah game.

▼ During the Passover seder, certain foods are eaten, in a particular order. Each of the foods has a special meaning.

hurry, and bitter herbs are eaten as a reminder of the bitterness of slavery.

Sukkot

The Sukkot festival begins five days after Yom Kippur and lasts for seven days. It is a joyous and happy festival that commemorates the 40 years the Jewish people spent wandering in the desert after they fled Egypt. It is also a harvest festival. During the harvest, people stayed in temporary

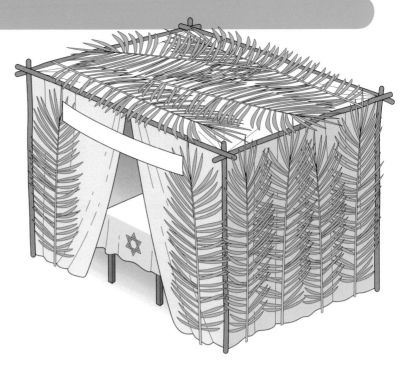

▲ During sukkot, many families build sukkoh in their gardens and decorate them with harvest foods. Some families also eat their meals outside in the sukkoh (singular form of sukkot).

► During Purim, children and adults dress up in costumes and attend a fete at the synagogue.

shelters, also called sukkot. Today, many families build sukkot in their gardens and eat their meals in them during this time.

Purim (Feast of Esther)

This fun festival remembers a story told in the Jewish Bible of how a Jewish woman called Esther, who lived in Persia in the 5th century BCE, saved the lives of all the Jews in Persia.

In the synagogue, the part of the Jewish Bible that tells the story of Esther is read out loud. Everyone dresses in costumes and hisses or boos whenever the villain's name (Haman) is mentioned. There may also be a community parade and fair, and gifts of food are given to the family and to the poor.

29

Weblink: www.CurriculumVisions.com

Glossary

ABRAHAM One of the patriarchs of Judaism. He was the first person to make a covenant with God.

AMIDAH A prayer that is the centre of any Jewish religious service. Also known as the Shemoneh Esrei or the Tefillah. The word amidah means standing and the prayer is recited while standing.

ANGEL A being created by God to carry God's messages to humans.

ARK A shorter way of saying Aron Kodesh (see below).

ARON KODESH The cabinet where the Torah scrolls are kept in the synagogue. The words Aron Kodesh are Hebrew for Holy Cabinet.

BABYLON A powerful ancient kingdom in what is modern day Iraq.

BCE This abbreviation stands for 'before common era'. This is another way of writing BC, or 'before Christ', when talking about dates.

BIMAH The raised platform from which the Torah is read during services.

CANAAN The ancient name of the land that God promised to the Israelites.

CANTOR The Yiddish word for chazan. Yiddish was a language spoken by European Jews.

CE This abbreviation stands for 'common era'. This is another way of writing AD, when talking about dates.

COMMANDMENT A rule or law. Judaism teaches that God gave the Jews 613 commandments, which Jews must follow.

COVENANT A binding agreement.

DIASPORA Any place outside of the land of Israel where Jews live. Diaspora refers to the fact that Jews were dispersed from ancient Israel by the Romans after the last Jewish revolt. The Hebrew term for this is 'galut'.

EXODUS A book of the Bible which describes how the Israelites fled from slavery in Egypt and wandered in the desert for 40 years.

FIVE BOOKS OF MOSES The first five books of the Bible. According to Jewish tradition, they were given to Moses by God.

GEMARA Commentaries on the Mishnah. The Mishnah and Gemara together make up the Talmud.

HALAKHAH Jewish law. The complete body of rules and practices that Jews are bound to follow, including Biblical commandments, commandments instituted by the rabbis and binding customs.

HAVDALAH A prayer ritual marking the end of Shabbat or a holiday. It consists of prayers said over a glass of wine, a candle and spices (cloves, cinnamon and bay leaves).

HEBREW The language spoken by the ancient Jews and the language of modern Israel. Jewish people are sometimes referred to as Hebrews or Hebrew people.

HOLOCAUST The killing of 6 million Jews (and other types of people deemed undesirable) by the Nazis in an attempt to destroy all Jewish people.

IDOL An image (a statue or painting, for example) of a god or goddess.

ISRAEL Modern Israel became a state in 1948, following a UN vote in 1947. It is roughly similar in area to ancient Israel.

ISRAELITE In ancient times, this referred to any descendant of Jacob (Israel). The ancient Jewish people were all descendants of Jacob, or Israelites.

JEW A person who follows the Jewish faith, or any person whose mother was a Jew or who converted to Judaism.

JUDAISM The religion of the Jewish people.

JUDEA The ancient Roman name for the land of ancient Israel.

KASHRUT Jewish dietary laws.

KIDDUSH A prayer recited over wine which sanctifies (makes holy) Shabbat or a holiday.

KIPPAH The skullcap head covering worn by Jewish men during services, and by some Jews at all times.

KOSHER Describes food that is permissible to eat under Jewish dietary laws. Can also describe any other ritual object that is fit for use according to Jewish law.

MAGEN DAVID Hebrew for Star of David or Shield of David. The six-pointed star emblem which is a common symbol of Judaism.

MENORAH A candelabrum. It usually refers to a seven or nine-branched candelabrum in the synagogue, or a seven-branched candelabrum used during Chanukkah.

MEZUZAH A case attached to the doorposts of houses, containing a scroll with passages of scripture written on it.

MIDDLE EAST The modern name for the region of the world where the ancient Israelites lived.

MISHNAH A written version of Jewish oral tradition, the basis of the Talmud.

MITZVOT (singular: **MITZVAH**) This means commandment, or any of the 613 commandments that Jews are obligated to observe. It can also mean any good deed.

NER TAMID A candelabrum or lamp near the Ark in the synagogue. It is always kept lit as a reminder that God's light is always near us.

ORAL TORAH Jewish teachings explaining the Written Torah, handed down orally until the 2nd century CE, when they began to be written down in what became the Talmud.

PATRIARCH The forefathers of Judaism – Abraham, Isaac and Jacob.

PROMISED LAND The land of Israel, which God promised to Abraham and his descendants.

PROPHET A spokesman for God, chosen to convey a message or teaching. Prophets were role models of holiness, scholarship and closeness to God.

RABBI A religious teacher and person authorised to make decisions on issues of Jewish law.

SHABBAT The Jewish day of rest. It runs from sundown on Friday to sundown Saturday.

SHEMA One of the most important and basic Jewish prayers. This consists of Deuteronomy 6:4–9, Deuteronomy 11:13–21 and Numbers 15:37–41.

SHEMONEH ESREI Another name for the Amidah prayer. The blessings of the Shemoneh Esrei can be broken down into three groups: blessings praising God, requests (forgiveness, redemption, health, prosperity and so on), and expressing gratitude and taking leave.

SHOAH The Hebrew word for the Holocaust.

SHOFAR A ram's horn, blown like a trumpet as a call to repentance on Rosh Hoshanah.

SIDDUR A prayer book, containing all the Jewish prayers.

SYNAGOGUE The Jewish house of worship.

TALLIT A prayer shawl which is worn during morning services.

TALMUD The written version of the Oral Torah.

TANAKH The Jewish Bible, what non-Jews call the Old Testament. The word is an acronym of Torah (Law), Nevi'im (Prophets) and Ketuvim (Writings).

TEN COMMANDMENTS The central laws given to Moses by God.

TEN PLAGUES To convince the Pharaoh to let the Israelite slaves leave Egypt, God sent ten plagues to Egypt: blood, frogs, lice, flies, cattle disease, boils, hail, locusts, darkness, death of all the Egyptian first-born.

THE TEMPLE The central place of worship in ancient Jerusalem, where sacrifices were offered.

TORAH Torah refers to both the first five books of the Bible, sometimes called the Pentateuch, and to the entire body of Jewish teachings.

YAD A hand-shaped pointer used while reading from Torah scrolls.

Index

Curriculum Visions

Curriculum Visions is a registered trademark of Atlantic Europe Publishing Company Ltd.

Dedicated Web Site
Watch movies, see many more pictures and read more about Judaism at:

www.curriculumvisions.com

(It's my turn! and the Learning Centre are subscription areas of the web site)

A CVP Book © 2005–2010
Atlantic Europe Publishing

First reprint 2007. Second reprint 2010.

The rights of Brian Knapp and Lisa Magloff to be identified as the authors of this work have been asserted by them in accordance with the Copyright, Designs and Patents Act 1988.

All rights reserved. No part of this publication may be reproduced, stored in a retrieval system, or transmitted in any form or by any means, electronic, mechanical, photocopying, recording or otherwise, without prior permission of the publisher and copyright holders.

Authors
Brian Knapp, BSc, PhD, and Lisa Magloff, MA

Religious Adviser
Valerie Boyd-Hellner

Art Director
Duncan McCrae, BSc

Senior Designer
Adele Humphries, BA

Acknowledgements
The publishers would like to thank the following for their help and advice:
The Hendon Reform Synagogue, London.

Photographs
The Earthscape Picture Library, except page 24 *The Granger Collection, New York.*

Illustrations
David Woodroffe

Designed and produced by
Atlantic Europe Publishing

Printed in China by
WKT Company Ltd

Jewish faith and practice
– *Curriculum Visions*
A CIP record for this book is available from the British Library

Paperback ISBN 978 1 86214 466 8

This product is manufactured from sustainable managed forests. For every tree cut down at least one more is planted.